D0771029

betty and rita LA DOLCE VITA

PHOTOGRAPHS BY Michael Malyszko

TEXT BY Judith E. Hughes

CHRONICLE BOOKS
SAN FRANCISCO

Text copyright © 2001 by Judith E. Hughes.
Photographs copyright © 2001 by Michael Malyszko.
All rights reserved. No part of this book may be reproduced in
any form without written permission from the publisher.

Library of Congress Cataloging-in-Publication Data available.

ISBN 0-8118-3198-1

Printed in Hong Kong.

Distributed in Canada by Raincoast Books
9050 Shaughnessy Street
Vancouver, BC V6P 6E5

10 9 8 7 6 5 4 3 2 1

Chronicle Books LLC
85 Second Street
San Francisco, California 94105

www.chroniclebooks.com

This time it's *mille grazie* to Betty, who stoically underwent two major surgeries in the fall of 1999 and came back panting for another trip abroad.

Hey, look at us two: we're Betty and Rita,

who went off to search for *la dolce vita*

in the beautiful city of Rome.

We skipped and we ran. We were hounds far from home.

Down *l'Appia Antica* we started to roam

and hurried our paws quite a lot.

The Romans were clever with water they brought

through this *acquedotto.* We paused and we caught

our breath in a park with no name.

L'Arco di Tito was built to proclaim

the emperor's deeds and ensure that his fame
in history surpassed all the others.

La Lupa is known as the first Roman mother,

who served as wet nurse to the city's first brothers, here carved in a fine piece of stone.

As time inches forward, a lot gets redone,

for instance the ancient site *il Pantheon,*

which now is a burial place.

Il cambio della guardia sets a dull pace

with a band and some soldiers and a fence in our face.

The march was incredibly slow.

Il Vittoriale is quite tough to show.
It's really too big for a proper photo,

so we featured our bodies instead.

Piazza Navona's the place, it is said,

for amateur art before off you might head

in search of a succulent treat.

With this in our minds, we then jogged 'cross this street

in search of a good meal, some *pasta* and meat

and with luck maybe even a *dolce.*

Still looking for food, it was late in the day,
when Rita got scared and then took off away.

Le moto had zoomed past too near.

Come on, Betty, *pronto.* Let's get out of here.

Il traffico's noisy. To me it's quite clear:

we need to go to someplace new.

Now I'm off and running; I can't wait for you.

I think that this *scala* should lead somewhere. Whew!

Perhaps, after all, this will work.

But streets without sidewalks seemed destined to irk,

especially when *gatti* like these you see lurk
and leer out from under each car.

Wherever I went I saw *"SPQR"*

and though I kept running, I never got far

away from this *motto* of Rome.

Beginning to fear that I'd never find home,

I found a *fontana* and drank with aplomb,

but felt I could still use some food.

With Rita long gone, you might think it was rude

to scarf down a *pizza,* though that was my mood—

as a dog, it's what I had to do.

With a need to digest, I went for a view

atop *il Gianicolo,* where I could chew

any old stick on the ground.

Il dolce far niente had me lying down

to take a brief doze on a statue I'd found   with fantastic, huge marble toes.

Well rested, I thought I would shop for some clothes

and went to the district and pressed up my nose

to *la finestra di Fendi.*

For my part, I hoped that *la moda* would send me off on adventures, but windows this trendy

made me feel lost and alone.

La notte descending, and scared to the bone,

I went off to sleep in a dark catacomb.

Tomorrow I'd look for my friend.

Trastevere's where I wound up at day's end,

in hopes that poor Rita'd be round the next bend

instead of an empty church square.

I'd heard *Aventino*'s weird keyhole was where

St. Peter's was framed, so I offered a prayer.

Ignored! What a feeble pretext!

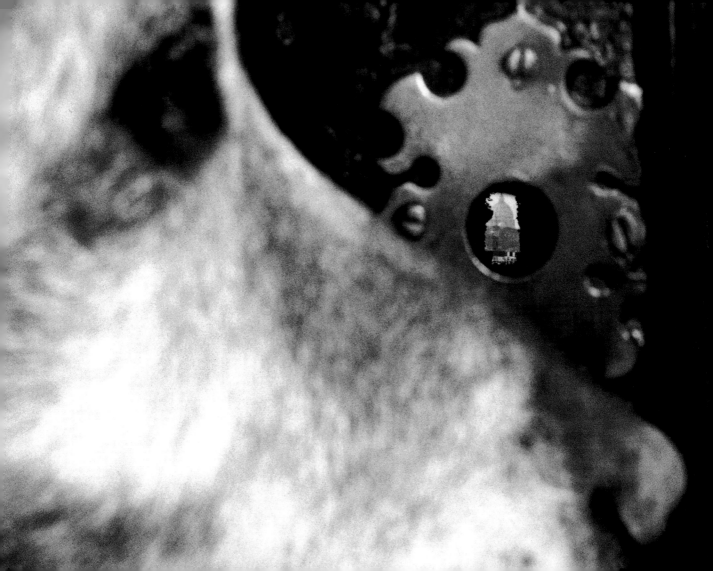

La nicchia della madonna was next.

Though I'm not religious, I didn't expect
to be left with no answer to "Where?"

This classic *cartello* told me to "Beware of the Dog," but, quite desperate, I didn't care.

I would take any suggestion.

The pooch in the courtyard replied to my question,

"Of all *le piazze, Campidoglio*'s the best one.

From there, I am sure you will see her."

At *il Circo Massimo* the real Roman curs

all agreed once they'd had a chance to confer.

They said, *"Spagna*'s the place to go!"

Up on the high ground, I felt good on *il Pincio,*

from where I could scan all the tourists below.

Per fortuna, my Betty was there!

"Hey! *Che incosciente!* I've looked everywhere!"

Together again, it seemed stupid to care.
We decided to get a bit blotto.

Italy's quite famous for its *gelato.*

We tried many flavors but chose *cioccolato*

as best, giving in to this whim!

We cooled ourselves off with a quick little swim,

but *i Carabinieri* caught us jumping in   and made us jump out just as quick.

At *Villa Borghese,* we grabbed a short stick

and played tug-of-war and took a neat pic
of us imitating a statue.

Cinecittà was our next photo venue

where Betty played *diva,* and I ingenue,

'cause the shades wouldn't stay on my cheeks!

This group of *monache* played great hide-and-seek.

In black, little Rita hid well, 'til I peeked,

which made my friend very annoyed.

In Rome *le rovine* are hard to avoid.

The old and the new are so often alloyed,

and medieval and ancient unite.

The legend suggests that *la Bocca* will bite   the hand of a liar. We tested its might

by telling a lie that was small.

L'elefantino by *Bernini* is tall.

We perched high on ledges and tried not to fall

to capture the photo we wanted.

In Rome *una bella figura* is flaunted

when making *la passeggiata.* Undaunted,

we nakedly joined the parade.

In *il Colosseo* the Romans had played

some dangerous games, but we weren't afraid.

Together, we knew we had won.

La Fontana di Trevi: our last stop for fun.

We made a few wishes to come back here soon,

tossing in coins by the light of the moon.

Afterword

When our publisher graciously offered us the opportunity to do a sequel to *Betty and Rita Go to Paris*, we seized on Rome, almost from the outset. Here is a city filled with historical icons yet teeming with life, steeped in romantic classicism but loved just as dearly for its food, its wine, its people. Besides, we hadn't been there in almost two decades!

So, March 2000 found us ensconced in a tiny apartment in the oldest part of the Eternal City. *Il Colosseo* loomed next door to us, and we crossed over the Imperial Fora almost every day on our explorations. The hideous but hugely visible *Vittoriale* often guided us home those first days, when, reliant on maps and our developing Italian, we were often lost. But no matter: there was always *gelato* or *pizza* around every corner, and the weather was mild and sunny for so early in the season.

People often ask if the dogs know that they are being photographed. After Rome we can say most assuredly, "Yes." Again they rose to each occasion to wander the streets with enthusiasm, even though, this time with a more pressing schedule, our days were often ten hours and five miles long. In Rome, they found ways to tell us when they felt we had gotten the shot: Betty would melt onto the sidewalk into a graceful curve of repose, while Rita would run towards the camera barking, *"Basta !"*

Our month in Rome was of course replete with characters and stories enough to fill a book: our landlord, who thought the dogs stayed on the terrace when we left them in the apartment (they slept on the couch); the number of images achieved in the first few frames, despite rolls and rolls shot trying to perfect the shots; and Michael elbowing his way to the forefront of a small army of tourists busily taking *our* photograph.

Once again we have many people to thank for their help in making this book become a reality. Barbara DiFerrante, a stateside friend, put us in contact with her host of Roman cousins and friends. Her cousin Vittorio Coronati not only wined and dined us one of our first nights in the city, but also helped us straighten out our internet connections (vital to a viable home away from home). Our producer Riccardo used his charm and good looks to get us inside several key monuments, then repaid us with a hair-raising car tour of the outskirts of the city! The caretakers of the Pantheon and the catacombs, who bent the rules to let the dogs inside, shall remain nameless but not thankless. The *terza rima* rhyme scheme benefited greatly from the patient guidance of our friend and poet, Mary Jo Salter. The impeccable hand-processing of Michael's film by the *Laboratorio Evangelisti e Corvaglia* made pleasurable work of the final printing in Boston. Finally, a special thank you to our daughter Maeve who, rallying against teenage tendencies, got up early in the morning and walked the streets of Rome to the point of exhaustion to help us.

FINE.